1 Edinburgh: the Castle from the Grassmarket, 1878

2 *Overleaf* 'The Covenanter', this photograph was originally captioned, and certainly the figure it illustrates belongs to an ageless aspect of the Lowlands (*c*. 1905)

Victorian and Edwardian

SCOTTISH
LOWLANDS

from historic photographs

Introduction and commentaries by

IAN DONNACHIE and INNES MACLEOD

B.T. BATSFORD LTD
LONDON

For Lowlanders everywhere

. . . I need
No world more spacious than the region here:
. . .
The villages that sleep the winter through,
And, wakening with the spring, keep festival
All summer and all autumn: this grey town
That pipes the morning up before the lark
With shrieking steam, and from a hundred stalks
Lacquers the sooty sky; where hammers clang
On iron hulls, and cranes in harbours creak
Rattle and swing, whole cargoes on their necks;
Where men sweat gold that others hoard or spend,
And lurk like vermin in their narrow streets:
This old grey town, this firth, the further strand
Spangled with hamlets, and the wooded steeps,
Whose rocky tops behind each other press,
Fantastically carved like antique helms
High-hung in heaven's cloudy armoury,
Is world enough for me.

JOHN DAVIDSON (1857–1909), *Ballads and Songs*, 1894

First published 1979
Text ©I. Donnachie & I. Macleod 1979

ISBN 0 7134 1297 6

Filmset in 'Monophoto' Apollo by
Servis Filmsetting Ltd, Manchester
Printed in Great Britain by
The Anchor Press Ltd, Tiptree, Essex
for the Publishers B.T. Batsford Ltd
4, Fitzhardinge Street, London W1A 0AH

3 On the beach, Portobello, 1907

CONTENTS

ACKNOWLEDGMENTS

Our efforts in selecting material for this volume would have been both less fruitful and less pleasurable without the help and encouragement of the following people and organisations:

Aberdeen University Library; Jim Arnold, New Lanark; Miss J. Christie and Mrs. J. Jaffray, National Monuments Record of Scotland; Mr. B. Lambie, Biggar; Mr. Lidster, Peebles; Mrs. Manson, Portincaple; Mrs. Taylor, Glasgow; Captain MacShannon, Campbeltown; Mrs. Munro, Glasgow; Mr. S. Macmillan, Rothesay; Joanna Mundy, Perth Museum and Art Gallery; Paisley Museum and Art Gallery; Dr. M. Robson, Hawick; St. Andrews University Library; Rev. W. Sinclair Armstrong, Newton Stewart; Mr. Tracey, Rothesay.

For permission to reproduce photographs we are grateful to:

Bute and District Library 103, 104, 105
Mr. A. Campbell, Kirkcudbright 48, 69, 71, 72, 73
Mr. R. Clapperton, Selkirk 29, 95
Mr. Collin, Stewartry Museum, Kirkcudbright 25, 26, 83
The Headmaster, Craigflower School, Fife 66
Mrs. Gladstone of Capenoch, Dumfries-shire 67
Gladstone Court Museum, Biggar 27, 57, 70, 107
Museum and Art Gallery, Hawick 15, 16, 56, 58, 93, 94, 95
Mr. J. McDavid, Creetown 77, 79, 82
National Monuments Record of Scotland, Royal Commission on The Ancient & Historical Monuments of Scotland 21, 22, 24, 31, 36, 37, 42, 44, 45, 47, 49, 53, 61, 62, 63, 64, 65, 68, 91, 92, 100, 110, 112
North Berwick Museum 63
New Lanark Conservation and Civic Trust 76, 78
Mr. Parker Love, Kilbirnie, Ayrshire 22, 110
Mr. G. Paul, Carnwath 55, 80
Perth Museum and Art Gallery 13, 14, 18, 54, 81, 86
Miss Purdie, Newton Stewart 97, 98
Mrs. Shepherd, Campbeltown 102
St. Andrews Preservation Trust 31, 42, 112
Mr. J. Tweedie, Currie 17

Photographs not otherwise acknowledged are from the compilors' and publisher's own collections.

A special word of thanks is due to Aileen Arnot, who typed this book.

INTRODUCTION

Most Scots and descendants of earlier emigrants to all corners of the globe regard themselves as either Highlanders or Lowlanders. The Lowlands are perhaps more difficult to define than the Highlands since the latter remain closely identified with remnants of the old Gaelic culture, while the former have been exposed to many external influences over the centuries. Stretching from the Borders to the Highland Line, the Lowlands encompass a vast area of regional diversity, a variety of scene from the rolling Border hills, moorlands and rocky shores of Galloway, the magnificent waters and islands of the Firth of Clyde, the rich farmlands of the Lothians, Fife and Angus, the industrial heartland of Lanarkshire, to the Highland foothills and glens of Perthshire. Although dominated by the great conurbations around Glasgow and Edinburgh, the Lowlands is essentially an area of smaller towns and villages – and of great expanses of fine farming countryside fringed with coastal settlements, reaching on the east from Berwick to Stonehaven, and on the west from the Solway Firth to Southern Argyll. This book includes photographs drawn from a wide area and covers the new regions of Strathclyde, Lothian, Fife, Tayside, Central, Borders and Dumfries and Galloway.

From the 1840s onwards a growing army of photographers and their assistants were recording the Scottish Lowland scene. The material they produced is now recognised as having a truly special value as an image of Victorian and Edwardian life.

Photographs really can capture something of the essence of the past, of the quality of life, even if like all source material, collections can be misused. It is quite possible to turn visual evidence into a propaganda exercise in the tradition of 'gloom, grime and girning'; or to produce a trivialisation, filling up pages with plates of elderly 'characters' whereas in fact the populace was predominantly youthful and vigorous. It is not easy to strike a balance. Indeed it is all too easy to produce a supposedly arcadian rural life as compared to the urban experience of Glasgow and Greenock, a life where all is serenity and sweetness and where hard work and sobriety were rewarded with success and a dignified old age. Life in general was always far rougher and coarser than most collections can suggest.

There were far more photographers than might be supposed. Recent studies have shown the importance of the work of the pioneering calotypists David Octavius Hill and Robert Adamson in Edinburgh between 1843 and 1848 and Thomas Rodger in St. Andrews. It is much more difficult to assess the work of the full-time and part-time photographers in the 1850s and 1860s who, either working from their shops or homes or travelling the countryside to set up booths ('photographic galleries') at local fairs and markets, brought the new technology and the new art form to the people. A good deal of rivalry sometimes existed between them, as these Biggar notices suggest:

Portraits
Mr. McPherson has been induced to remain in Biggar for a few weeks longer, and will continue take Portraits till about the middle of April. Portraits on Glass and Leather. Brooches and Locke Fitted. Charges Moderate. Photographic Gallery, Biggar, 1st April 1859.

Portraits
Real Striking Likenesses. M. Moffat has been induced to remain at his residence, Hartree Ga for some time longer. Portraits from One Shilling Upwards. Brooches, Lockets, Pins, Rings, et Fitted. Hartree, May 2, 1859.

By the later nineteenth century the studios of the great professional photographers, Valentine of Dundee and G.W. Wilson of Aberdeen, were very extensive business employing a great many people and operating throughout the U.K. (indeed by the 188 G.W. Wilson had units in Europe, Australia and Africa). Some town businesses, such as . Brown & Co. of Lanark, worked throughout Scotland, and others, for example C. Reid Wishaw, on a county basis. And there were the small country photographers operati more or less on their own, men like J.P. Milnes of Stranraer, Hunter of Newton Stewa McConchie of Kirkcudbright, and Brownlee of Portpatrick, who produced work of supe quality.

The 1881 Census Table of Occupations in Scotland lists 953 working photographers. Tl 1891 Census lists 1,826 (1,017 men and 809 women). Many of them, of course, we workshop assistants and general employees. The 1891 County list includes:

Aberdeenshire 214 (including Aberdeen 174)
Angus 231 (Dundee 176)
Perthshire 33   East Lothian 3
Fife 79   Berwickshire 4
Stirlingshire 26   Peebles-shire 2
Dunbartonshire 35   Selkirkshire 11
Renfrewshire 103   Roxburghshire 20
Ayrshire 66   Dumfries-shire 22
Lanarkshire 516 (Glasgow 399)   Stewartry of Kirkcudbright 3
Midlothian 306 (Edinburgh 261)   Wigtownshire 5
West Lothian 4

In addition there were the part-time professional photographers (otherwise making living as tailors, cabinetmakers, joiners, architects, etc.), probably more in the peri before the later 1880s when cameras became cheaply available for the first time. Moreover there were undoubtedly many aristocratic and middle class amateur photographers whose work is only gradually being recognised and identified. Lady Henrietta Gilmour Montrave was a highly gifted, indeed expert, photographer (plates 53, 61). Her family seems to have been one of many in country houses who took a practical interest in the use of the camera. How many mansions had their own studios and equipment such as those indicated in this advertisement?

> Residence to let in the Parish of Borgue . . . for one year . . . the Mansion House of Senwick . . . first rate Offices, consisting of Workshop and Photographic Dark Room, Six-Stalled Stable and large Coach-House . . . Asphalt Lawn Tennis Court . . .
> (*Kirkcudbrightshire Advertiser*, 3 June 1892)

In the West of Scotland William Edward Griffin, secretary to Wm. Graham & Co., turned out a series of prints recording family life in Glasgow, Ayrshire and Dumfries-shire of a consistently high quality. Some of his street scenes are beautifully composed and lively examples capturing essential qualities of life in the 1900s. Moreover he also produced some very special photographs – in particular his study (plate 23) of his mother, Mrs. Isabella Griffin, neé Aitken, of Edinburgh, and his wife, Mademoiselle Angèle Duringe of Paris, at the family summer house, Antrim Cottage at Prestwick, in 1902. Here the photographer is very much the creative artist and technologist at the same time.

LOWLAND PROSPECT

4 Victorian architectural grandeur at its best, seen here in the splendid facade of Greenock General Post Office, about 1890

5 Brechin from the bridge, about 1880. This photograph by the George Washington Wilson studio shows a skyline of chimneys rising from the local linen mills. Judging from the crowd, which always seemed to turn up when the early photographers were setting up their apparatus, this was shot on a holiday or at the weekend. Some of the houses in the middle background are built with their gable-ends facing the street – an architectural feature often found in Lowland towns and villages

6 A sunny harbourside scene at Gourock, one of the principal ports of call for Clyde steamers sailing 'Doon the Water'. No doubt there was plenty to interest this group of the boys in and around the pier and nearby railway station

7 *Above* shows the Aberdeen Express travelling northwards across the Forth Bridge on a day in 1905 – some 15 years after the bridge had been completed

8 Dalintober Quay, Campbeltown, Argyll, about 1890, a familiar scene to thousands of summer visitors and day trippers from Glasgow and other Clyde ports. In the background is a group of recently constructed villas that command a fine view of the bay. Notice the fishing nets hung up to dry, and on the left beside the little boy in traditional sailor's suit, an old cast-iron stand pipe

9 The Whitesands, Dumfries, about 1890, probably on the occasion of a weekly market. Sheep, horses and cattle are for sale by auction and the area is a hive of activity. Undoubtedly the many pubs and hotels did good business on market days like this. Points of special interest include a span of the ancient Devorgilla's Bridge (right), the Old Dock on the River Nith (centre, beyond the cattle), and the chimneys of local tweed mills. Cloth-making was once as important in Dumfries as it remains today in the Borders

10 The famous 'Tam O' Shanter Inn', Ayr, photographed about 1890. A statuette of the poet, Robert Burns, can be seen in the window to the left of the door

11 The Town Hall and riverside square, Paisley, seen here about the turn of the century. Paisley's prosperity was built on thread manufacture and many of the town's finest buildings were raised by mill-owners, like the Coats family. Note the electric trams and bridge over the River Cart

12 Crail in the East Neuk of Fife, a popular spot with artists and photographers to the present day, is shown here about 1885. The definition in the original photograph by George Washington Wilson is superb. A ketch is berthed in the harbour, while smaller fishing boats can be seen near the harbour entrance. Notice the gas work with its retort house and chimney. Gas works were often built as near sea-level as possible to allow the maximum atmospheric pressure to act on the holder. The vernacular architecture is typical of much of the Eastern Lowlands, and many of the houses seen here have been restored with the encouragement of the National Trust for Scotland

COUNTRY LIFE

In terms of area the Lowlands of Scotland are essentially rural in character, and this was even more true in Victorian and Edwardian times than it is today. From Angus in the north-east to Wigtownshire in the south-west the Lowlands encompassed a widespread farming community still dominated by the old landed gentry, who had controlled their estates and much else besides for generations. Despite overall population decline in rural areas, and a notable drift to the towns, village life was still generally vibrant. Even by the 1870s the railway had not penetrated everywhere and the limitations of horse transport meant that there was still a considerable local demand for the skills provided by tradesmen like the blacksmith, millwright, joiner or saddler. Above all most villages of any consequence had a school, which at least kept children at home until they had received a basic education and had to leave for farm or other work at the ages of 12 or 13.

Dunning in Strathearn, Perthshire (see plates 13 and 14) was probably typical of hundreds of villages

13 *Previous page* and **14** *right* The cohesiveness of the typical Lowland village community is well illustrated in these two photographs of Dunning, Perthshire. The general view is of 1903, that of the square with its ornamental thorn tree may be earlier. The Norman-Romanesque tower of the Old Parish Church can be seen in both plates. The thorn tree is clearly the rendezvous of village worthies, though this particular shot shows a group of local children posed for the camera

15 *Below* Inns had an important social function in rural communities, as well as serving the passing trade. This one at Bonchester Bridge, Roxburghshire, photographed about 1890, clearly served both locals and travellers. The building next door, to the right of this picture was probably a smithy (see plate 16) and the horse pulling the wagonette nearest the camera might well have been taken in for shoeing at the blacksmith's forge

16 *Facing page* Blacksmith, customers and assorted onlookers at Cauldmill Smithy, Roxburghshire, captured in this photograph taken in 1886. The blacksmith served an important function in country communities for he built and repaired farm machinery as well as seeing to the horses. The usual range of tools, implements and scrap metal can be seen scattered around the building. Note the large door giving access to the work area where the forge is located

scattered throughout the Lowlands. In the 1890s, with a population of around 850 it was described as 'a small, neat, little place, and possesses a branch of the Union Bank, a local savings bank, inns, gas work, a town hall, a library and reading room, a mutual improvement society, bowling and curling clubs, and a co-operative society'. According to the *Ordnance Gazetteer*, 'a plentiful supply of water' had been introduced in 1872, and 'a magnificent fountain, the gift of a successful native abroad' was erected in the village square. The thorn tree (seen in plate 14) had been planted following the burning of the village during the first Jacobite Rising of 1715. Despite the decline of handloom weaving – a widespread activity throughout the Lowlands in the earlier part of the nineteenth century – Dunning maintained something of its former prosperity by serving the surrounding countryside as a market centre.

Craftsmen were still to be found in considerable numbers in country villages during the Victorian and Edwardian eras. Dunning, Currie, Kirkcolm and Lochwinnoch were all large enough to provide work for a wide range of tradesmen. Lochwinnoch in Renfrewshire (plates 22 and 24) with a population of 1,500 in 1891 combined agriculture and industry in a pattern common to much of the Lowlands. Likewise, Currie, Midlothian (plate 17) was an important centre of processing industries using the products of the land as their raw material. Both grain milling and leather tanning were old-established trades there. Kirkcolm, Wigtownshire (plate 19) was by comparison overwhelmingly rural in character, set in undulating farm land at the northern tip of the Rhinns of Galloway.

Social conditions in the countryside often left as much to be desired as those in the towns and cities. Farm and other labourers were still partly paid in kind and usually lived in tied cottages. A large proportion of girls and womenfolk were either employed on the farm or in domestic service. Life was probably most difficult for migrant harvest labourers, many of them Irish – and for the itinerant gypsies, some of whom are seen in photographs here.

17 Loading carts at Newmills Mill, Currie, Midlothian, in 1909. The miller, or perhaps his assistant, can be seen at the granary door on the first floor. Water mills producing oat meal or wheaten flour for local consumption were once common throughout the Lowlands.

18 Spittalfield sawmill and workshop near Blairgowrie, Perthshire, about 1880. Timber remained an important material in the construction of carts, wheels and all sorts of machinery long after the general introduction of iron. Judging from the confusion in the yard this looks like a general workshop for the construction and repair of anything that was needed by the local farming and village communities

19 Sleepy Kirkcolm village, Wigtownshire, captured here on a bright summer's morning by George Washington Wilson about 1890. Like many photographs of the period this has a somewhat artistic quality, reflected in the formal pose of the figures in the foreground. Kirkcolm, near the shore of Loch Ryan, is typical of hundreds of single-street villages throughout the Lowlands

20 An apparently delightful farmyard scene in this old but undated photograph shows the squalid housing conditions of the rural poor even in the second half of the nineteenth century.

21 A ford over the River Tyne at Haddington, East Lothian, about 1900. Fords were often the only means of crossing rivers in the countryside until the arrival of the motor car with its temperamental internal combustion engine necessitated the construction of bridges. Compare the scene here with that in plate **39**

22 Cattle Show Day, Lochwinnoch, an occasion which clearly brought all classes together to enjoy themselves. Judging from the number of bookmakers (right and centre) horse or perhaps foot races formed additional attractions. Calderhaugh Mill, an old silk and linen factory, can be seen in the background

23 A summer photograph of two ladies preparing blackcurrants for jam-making

24 Taken on a bright summer's day − the kind that must have been welcomed by the early photographers − this plate shows the main street of Lochwinnoch, Renfrewshire, probably on Cattle Show Day, about 1890 (see plate 22). Although Lochwinnoch was a textile manufacturing village of some importance farming remained the economic mainstay of the surrounding countryside − as it still is to this day. Notice the barefoot boys in the foreground and the little girls on stilts. Perhaps a race on stilts was being run at the show, along with other attractions for the children

25, 26 *Left* The tinker-gypsy camp at the Doon, near Kirkcudbright, about 1900. The travelling folk were regarded with more respect and tolerance in the countryside, than the usual fear and suspicion they encountered in the town. These summer scenes undoubtedly show the more idyllic aspects of gypsy life

27 *Above* Another gypsy camp at Biggar, Lanarkshire, in the summer of 1906. Notice the group of amateur sociologists, bottom right

28 Washday Blues! Like the old 'Covenanter' seen in plate 2 washday scenes were popular subjects with photographers, often for use as post-cards. This one by Valentine dates from the turn of the century

29 End of an era! A portable threshing mill and steam engine at work somewhere in the Borders. Mills of this kind travelled from farm to farm at harvest time and were later replaced by combine-harvesters. Notice the water cart for supplying the engine

0 A Valentine photograph of Dockhead Street, Saltcoats in 1896. Judging from
he crowd this was either taken on a local market day or, more likely, on Fair
aturday, since Saltcoats was always a popular spot with Glasgow trippers.
otice again the numerous children, the ornate shopfronts with blinds drawn
gainst the sunlight, a proliferation of trade signs, and the old oil-lamp bracket
ove the doorway in the left foreground

Although dominated by the great urban centres of Glasgow, Edinburgh and to some lesser extent Dundee, the Scottish Lowlands is predominantly an area of small burghs, industrial and market towns. Fairs or markets were regular – often weekly – events, and sometimes attracted crowds from all over the country. Photographers captured the bustle of such scenes at Falkirk (plate 32), Arbroath (plate 33) and Dumfries (plates 34, 35). In many instances craft and industrial activities were essentially related to the needs of the surrounding countryside, hence the growth of trades like building, agricultural engineering and farm processing.

Lanark (plate 43) is typical of many Lowland burghs, both for its setting in the rural Upperward of Clydesdale and for its mixture of farming and industrial activities. The town grew rapidly during the nineteenth century. Its population had risen to over 7,500 in 1881, by which time the place was said to possess 'so many amenities in itself and such full command of its beautiful environs, as to be both a very agreeable place of residence and a crowded resort of summer tourists'. Nearby was the industrial village of New Lanark (plate 44) where water power from the River Clyde had been harnessed to drive cotton spinning machinery during the classic Industrial Revolution.

The photographs of Glasgow, Edinburgh and Dundee show familiar street scenes – as they were – in late Victorian or Edwardian times. Like most of the plates in this section of the book they tend to convey an impression of bustle and prosperity, though undeniably there was as much poverty and hardship in the cities as in the countryside. The Glasgow and Edinburgh closes, with all their overcrowding and disease, were rarely photographed, and then only when civic improvement had removed the most obvious aspects of their squalor.

31 'News from Afar', a posed but none the less artistic photograph taken in St Andrews about 1860, shows the local postman making a delivery to a fisherman's family. The little girl at the top of stair has moved while the photograph was being taken. Traditional fish baskets can be seen at the bottom of the steps

32 Typical of many industrial towns in the Lowlands, Falkirk, seen here, still retained its links with the countryside through the monthly 'trysts' or cattle fairs. This photograph of the High Street, about the turn of the century, was probably taken on such an occasion. The old Town Steeple, dating from 1813, resembles that of Lanark (see plate 43). Notice on the right an ironmonger's shop with its wares strung up at all angles by the door

33 'Feeing Saturday', Arbroath, seen
in a photograph by Geddes & Son,
about 1900. Four times a year a
'Feeing Market' – a sort of informal
labour exchange for farm servants,
byremen, shepherds, and ploughmen
– was held in the main streets of
Arbroath. It was clearly the occasion
for a general holiday and fair, as the
great throng here indicates

34, 35 Ancient and modern are seen in these two photographs of Dumfries taken about 1890. The street beneath the Old Tolbooth (or gaol) serves both as a meeting place and an informal market, while another nearby focal point is the splendid cast-iron fountain. A horse bus can just be seen disappearing along the street on the right

36, 37 *Left* Two views of Princes Street and Calton Hill, Edinburgh. In the upper photograph, taken by J. Patrick about 1890, the Scott Monument can be seen to advantage. Notice the cabs on the right and the horse-trams in the distance. The lower photograph, actually shot from the Scott Monument, shows Waverley Market with its roof-top gardens, *c.* 1895. The great dome of Register House is on the left, while the roof of the old Calton Jail is just visible on the right.

38 *Above* High Street, Dundee, seen here in a Valentine photograph taken about 1905. Dundee's prosperity in the Victorian era was built as much om commerce as on the traditional three 'J's' of Jute, Jam and Journalism with which the city was then so closely associated. In the foreground is the classical Town Hall, designed by the elder Adam, and in the near distance the lofty and beautiful spire of the Episcopal Cathedral of St Paul, erected from a design of the great nineteenth-century architect Sir Gilbert Scott

39 Jamaica Bridge, Glasgow in 1899 – a scene which captures all the bustle of city life in late Victorian times. Traffic was clearly becoming a problem, though electrification of the tramway system, begun in 1898 and completed four years later, undoubtedly helped to reduce the chaos. Notice the long line of carts heading for the city centre of the docks, and the massive iron bridge in the background carrying the Caledonian Railway over the River Clyde to Central Station. A riverside walkway has recently been constructed along the old quays seen beneath the bridges

40 *Above* George Square, Glasgow, photographed about 1875 by the George Washington Wilson studio. The graceful square with its gardens and Sir Walter Scott's statue as its centre-piece provides a warm and sunny spot for the citizens – ladies with parasols and behatted gentlemen. Hotels flank the north side of the square, one being the North British Hotel with the North British Railway Station (now Queen Street Station) immediately behind

41 *Left* Another fine George Washington Wilson photograph of a familiar corner, St Vincent's Place, Glasgow, headquarters of several famous Scottish shipping and insurance companies. An old horse tram – advertising 'Sunlight Soap' – can be seen behind the group of small boys posing for the camera

42 A close in St Andrews about 1870. Mother looks on while daughter wrings out the clothes. The washtub is seen on the left

43 Morning sunshine helps the photographer capture the atmosphere of Lanark, the former county-town of Lanarkshire and market for the Upperward of Clydesdale. In Victorian and Edwardian times Lanark was a popular resort, the principal attractions being the nearby Falls of Clyde and the orchard and fruit lands of the Clyde Valley. A niche above the entrance to the Old Steeple contains a massive and somewhat unedifying statue of the Scottish patriot, Sir William Wallace, who first raised his standard in the town

44 The village shop and staff at New Lanark, photographed about 1880. New Lanark, a cotton-spinning factory village on the River Clyde near Lanark, was established by David Dale in the 1780s and later made famous by his son-in-law, Robert Owen, the social reformer. At the time this photograph was taken the mills were owned by the Lanark Spinning Co., as the sign above the door proclaims. The barefoot boys contrast markedly with the impeccably dressed storemen. Recent work by the New Lanark Conservation Trust has restored the shopfronts exactly as they appear here

45 Pittenweem in Fife (1889), showing the East Shore and harbour. Beyond the web of sail and rigging on the left fishermen are at work mending nets, while other craftsmen are engaged in ship repair

BY THE SEA SHORE

No district of the Lowlands is far from the sea. Though there are only short reaches of navigable river, such as the Cart in Renfrewshire and the Nith in Dumfries-shire, the estuaries of the Clyde, Forth and Tay greatly facilitated transport and contributed to the growth of towns and industry during the nineteenth century. Even after the construction of railways in the Victorian era many coastal districts continued to depend on shipping as the main means of transport. Fishing was of long-standing importance along East and West coasts. Harbours, large and small, supported seafaring communities, engaged not only in fishing but also in a wide range of ancillary activities such as fish processing, sail, net and rope making.

Around the shores of the Forth were numerous fishing ports like Pittenweem, as seen here in plates 45 and 47. The old harbour, extended in 1855, had inner and outer basins but 'suffered from its small depth of water'. In 1893 the port had over 60 fishing boats employing 220 fishermen and boys, while fish gutting and curing provided work for the womenfolk and girls.

On the southern shore of the Forth the old port of Newhaven was as famous for its fishwives as for fish (plate 52). At the turn of the century the village still had an old fashioned air, and wrote one observer 'the red-tiled, two-storey houses, with outside stairs and jutting gables, and the big boats hauled up on the shore or rocking in the harbour all give it a picturesque look'. The fishwives with their heavy creels used to travel far and wide selling the catch.

Coastal shipping was of considerable importance in the south-west of Scotland even during Victorian times. Many of the old harbours along the shores of the Solway, such as Dalbeattie (plate 46) and Kirkcudbright (plate 48), were still used by sailing ships and steamers as late as 1914. The Galloway ports had long-established links with Cumbria and Lancashire, as well as with the Forth of Clyde to the north. Many of the harbours are now deserted, though a few, including Kirkcudbright, have recently been revived.

46 Dub O' Hass, the harbour of Dalbeattie on the River Urr, Kirkcudbrightshire, photographed about 1880. The main industry of Dalbeattie in Victorian times was granite-working at the nearby Craignair Quarries, the stone being shipped world-wide and used in prominent buildings and public works, like harbours and lighthouses. The photograph has been taken at high tide and the boat on the right appears to be unloading cargo on to waiting carts. Note the two men in a boat in the foreground!

47 Pittenweem harbour, about 1890. This photograph shows in the foreground two typical inshore boats of the period, and in the background vernacular buildings of the kind common in the older East Coast fishing villages and towns – from Eyemouth in the south to Stonehaven in the north. Note the artist with his easel and the onlookers: harbourside scenes like this one were popular with artists and photographers alike

48 *Left* An early photograph, taken about 1865, of the harbour and River Dee at Kirkcudbright. A steamship, probably the *Countess of Galloway*, which provided a regular service to Whitehaven and Liverpool from the Solway ports, can be seen in the Old Dock, now filled in and the site of a car park. In the foreground is the old ferry, while a variety of warehouses and the ruined Maclellan's Castle can be seen behind

49 *Right* An unusually fine photograph of a pleasure steamer at Aberdour, a popular resort on the Firth of Forth. In Victorian times regular steamship services were as much a feature of the Forth as in the Firth of Clyde, even after the opening of the great railway bridge in 1890. This photograph of trippers on the pier was probably taken about 1900, though it may be later

No. 2. On Campbeltown Quay. The Morning's Catch.

50 *Left On Campbelton Quay: The Morning's Catch* is the caption on this postcard of about 1910. The scene captures not only the camaraderie of the girls and women employed as fish gutters and packers, but also the drudgery of their occupation

51 *When the Boats Come In* — a widely reproduced photograph of an East Coast fisherman and child about the turn of the century

53 Two 'old salts' pose for Lady Henrietta Gilmour Montrave's camera at Montrose harbour in 1897. The harbour itself was built in 1843, the iron lock gates being operated by capstans, seen here. In the background a two-masted vessel has been pulled up on the patent slipway for repair

52 *Previous page* Four generations are represented in this family group posing at Newhaven about 1900. Family industry of this kind was common in the fishing villages around the shores of the Lowlands. Son followed father to the boats, while in mending nets, baiting the lines and selling the fish, daughter succeeded mother. Writing in 1853, Charles Reade recorded that the Newhaven fishwives had 'a grand corporal trait; they have never known a corset! So they are as straight as javelins; they can lift their hands above their heads. Their supple persons move as Nature intended; every gesture is ease, grace, and freedom'.

GETTING ABOUT

54 River Ferry on the Tay at Caputh near Dunkeld, Perthshire in the 1890s. A ferry float of this type was established in 1834. It consisted of a large platform upon two long narrow boats set parallel to each other. The chain across the river, passing over a fly-wheel at the side of the platform, kept the boat on a straight course

The nineteenth-century revolution in transport had an enormous impact upon the lives of the people of the Lowlands of Scotland (much of it was, indeed, their own achievement). They certainly shared the general and enormous Victorian enthusiasm for, and pride in, the engineering feats and the technological triumphs that had altered radically the possibilities of travel and trade and communication.

Yet the age of steamboats and great bridges, the age of railways and efficient public services, of the first motor buses and lorries and of motor cars as toys for the Edwardian rich and well-to-do was also still simultaneously a world of sailing ships and river ferries and toll houses. It remained still essentially at a local level a 'horse economy', dominated by and dependent upon horse-drawn carriages and carts. And for many of the poor pedestrianism remained a necessity.

55 Lampits Ferry Float on the Clyde between Pettinain and Carnwath: the ferryman, Andrew Cullen, with vanman Jimmy Grossart who worked for Smith, the Carnwath baker. Note the haystack on stilts in case of river flooding. The photograph was taken by J. Jackson, the Carnwath stationer, on 2 October, 1902

56 *Below* Dryburgh River Toll on the Tweed in Berwickshire, about 1890

57 The postman, J. Hogg, and cronies at Quothquan near Biggar, Lanarkshire about 1885. An irresistible photograph, even if it hardly suggests the efficiency of the British system for the collection and distribution of the mail. Their 'hostess', 'Easie' Watson, when challenged by the gaugers (i.e. excisemen) about the spirits she kept in her grandfather clock, replied 'What I gie, I gie, and what I git, I git'!

58 *Below* The Gordon Arms Hotel, Cappercleuch, St Mary's Loch, Selkirkshire. A well-patronised hostelry at a popular beauty spot for day trippers from Selkirk and Moffat

THOMSON & LAURIE'S
ROYAL AUCTION MART.

59, 60 Two Griffin photographs of commercial vehicles at the Whitesands, Dumfries about 1910. The former (*previous page*) outside Thomson and Laurie's Royal Auction Mart. The latter (*below*) including the New Bazaar Hotel, W.H.B. McKay's Harness and Saddlery Stores, Wallet's Auction Marts Office, and a surely over-loaded cart with a fine collection of basketry items

62 New Galloway Station, Mossdale, Stewartry of Kirkcudbright in the 1900s. The station was a long way from New Galloway. Transport includes an early Albion motor bus (SM 646), no doubt making for New Galloway, Dalry, Balmaclellan or Laurieston

61 *Right* Thornton Junction, Fife, 1895. Railway staff and passengers at an important local junction for the network of lines in Fife. For trains going south to Kirkcaldy, east to Methil, west to Dunfermline, and north to Markinch, Cupar and Perth. Photograph by Lady Henrietta Gilmour Montrave

63 A motor rally at Kilspindie near Aberlady, East Lothian in the 1900s. A concourse of mechanical and male elegance

UPSTAIRS, DOWNSTAIRS

64 The Ross, Hamilton, Lanarkshire
about 1890

One of the most obvious and important characteristics of the Victorian and Edwardian era in Lowland Scotland is the range of wealth and poverty, the extreme inequality and diversity of opportunity and experience and rewards that life could offer. So much in terms of future security and health and happiness depended on the accident of being born into a particular social class level.

The state of affairs may be seen in terms of four social classes: an upper class, including both the old landed aristocracy and new families whose wealth came from the Industrial Revolution; the middle class, with its especially sensitive gradations between the ranks of professional men and small businessmen and proprietors; the working class, urban and rural, including skilled and unskilled workers with the very different status and material rewards they enjoyed; and the poor and destitute, whether in the slums of Glasgow and Edinburgh or in tinker encampments in the countryside.

Photographs giving an excellent idea of the degree of carefully planned luxury, order and elegance possible for the upper class, and of the comfortable life enjoyed by the middle class are common in many

65 Overtoun House, near Dumbarton – the stable range with carriages and coachmen about 1890

collections. To support this comfort a huge staff of servants, coachmen, gardeners, gamekeepers and general estate workers was on hand, for example in 1881 the Census shows that there were 136,098 indoor servants and 11,258 domestic gardeners in Scotland. Domestic service, indeed, was the only career open for a great many girls and in general the supply far exceeded the demand in upper- and middle-class households. In contrast there were 53,741 coal miners and 31,785 working in the cotton industry in Scotland in 1881.

Few photographers showed an interest in working-class life. Curiously, the life of the more acutely poor and deprived, dependent on charity and totally lacking the privilege of privacy, was more likely to be recorded. Just occasionally special studies, such as Thomas Annan's *Old Closes and Streets of Glasgow* (1868–77), offer a detailed examination of the problems of the poor. But all too often they were turned into 'characters' or 'worthies', objects of curiosity for the patronising philanthropist and the middle-class tourist.

66 Croquet on the lawns at Craigflower House, Torryburn, Fife. A group photographed in 1896 by R.E. Croall and included in his family album

67 Household servants and estate staff, Capenoch House, by Thornhill, Dumfries-shire. Including the housekeeper, the cook, the butler, maids, gamekeepers, grooms and the coachman, foresters and gardeners. The employees of Thomas Stewart Gladstone, who died in 1882

68 Byreleehaugh, near Bellendean, west of Roberton, Roxburghshire. Rutherford, the Duke of Buccleuch's gamekeeper, and his estate cottage with thatched roof and water pump. The cottage was demolished in 1972. Photograph by Gaylor of Hawick

69 'The Kirkcudbright Artillery Volunteers.' No. 8 Company (Kirkcudbright), the Ayr and Galloway Artillery Volunteers, at the Battery at Sandside in the 1870s. Officers include Captain Shand (1813–95) and Lieut. Grierson. John Adolphus Shand and pony to the left. Photograph by W. Stewart of Kirkcudbright

70 *Right* C Company (Biggar), the 9th Lanarkshire Rifle Volunteers, in 1888. Sgt. Walter Lindsay, Sgt. Walter Rae, Sgt. John H. Wilson, Col. Sgt. Robert M. Dickson, and Sgt. John Eunson. The Corps then consisted of a Captain, two Lieutenants, a Sergeant Instructor, six Sergeants, five Corporals, four Lance Corporals, and 62 Privates. Photograph by Davidson and Son of Carluke and Lanark

71 David Ewart – 'decayed gentleman', Kirkcudbright, 1859

72 *Left, below* Dick Tyson – 'Englishman'. Innkeeper of the Selkirk Arms Hotel, Kirkcudbright. In earlier days a Cumberland pugilist, 1859

73 David McLellan – banker and later Town Clerk, Kirkcudbright. 1859. Absconded in October 1889 and charged in 1890 with having embezzled £1200 in $3\frac{1}{2}\%$ Blackburn Corporation Stock. 'Driven to Castle Douglas by George Scott, Dr. Reid's coachman – he never returned to Kirkcudbright.' Three portraits by W. Stewart of Kirkcudbright

RICH MAN, POOR MAN

74, 75 *Below and overleaf* Two family photographs by William Griffin. A middle class Glasgow family on holiday in Ayrshire. Very clever composition pieces expressing perfectly the prosperous and cheerful life possible for some in the Edwardian world

76 Another photograph of New Lanark about 1895, showing the mills with housing behind. Slaters are at work on top of the workshop roof in the foreground

78 New Lanark about 1895. The rounded end of Caithness Row (1792) in the centre background and the New Buildings (1798) on the left. Mill girls coming up from the mill. A rare effective photograph of working class life

77 *Right* Quarrymen near Creetown, Stewartry of Kirkcudbright, about 1885. With a massive granite block

79 *Left* 'A house built in a day.' Mr. and Mrs. Brown, Fell Quarries,
Creetown, about 1900. Photograph by W. Hunter of Newton Stewart

80 The Soup Kitchen, Carnwath, Lanarkshire, about 1900

CHILDREN AT WORK AND PLAY

81 Girls in a typical village street
scene at Shuttlefield, Newburgh, Fife
about 1903

Go around almost any village or town in the Lowlands today and the immediate impression is often how
many old people there are walking around and shopping. This is not merely an impression: it is a fact.
And one of the most striking differences between the Victorian and Edwardian period and our own
how very young the population as a whole was then – yet this is an aspect of the reigns of Victoria an
Edward VII often forgotten. Without labouring the point too much, it is perhaps interesting to wo
through some data from the 1891 Census of Scotland for a county (Ayrshire), an industrial town and po
(Greenock), a border town (Hawick), a small Lanarkshire town (Biggar), and a rural Perthshire pari
(Dunning). Undoubtedly it is the figures for Dunning that really brings this point home.

	AYRSHIRE	GREENOCK	HAWICK	BIGGAR	DUNNING
Under 5	30,345	8,424	1,708	232	128
5—	28,914	8,086	1,679	202	151
10—	27,101	7,696	1,715	184	146
15—	24,087	6,936	1,585	206	132
20—	19,581	6,180	1,289	146	103
25—	16,282	5,038	1,074	135	70
30—	14,189	4,516	987	123	80
35—	12,864	4,009	932	106	74
40—	10,873	3,688	766	108	59
45—	9,566	3,155	645	75	68
50—	8,432	2,766	570	71	68
55—	6,616	1,893	426	90	71
60—	6,016	1,615	341	61	47
65—	4,443	955	278	62	52
70—	3,407	685	203	55	43
75—	2,091	351	96	29	31
80 and over	1,579	254	54	17	22
Total	226,386	66,247	14,348	1,902	1,345

The children in the photographs sometimes seem to belong to our own jumble of dreams of how everyone would like to remember their childhood: so many of these photographs have a timeless, idyllic quality about them. Yet many of the children in them, from middle-class and prosperous working class families, can scarcely have enjoyed the discipline they endured and the formal clothes they had to wear. The girls, elaborately feminine in bonnets or hats, pinafores and petticoats and long stockings, bows and ribbons and long hair, and the boys, highly masculine in 'suits', waistcoats, jackets, caps, and heavy boots, were almost uniformly over-dressed. Even the poor, since they shared their cast-offs, look the same.

Life was a serious matter. Hard work, native ability, and a good education provided laudable opportunities for advancement socially and economically. At least this was the Scottish Lowland tradition, whatever difficulties may arise when the theory is applied to the urban masses of Glasgow and its neighbouring burghs. But there was a genuine and widespread enthusiasm for education in much of Lowland Scotland, a respect for distinctions achieved at school and (especially) at university and for the glory they brought to teachers, to parents and the extended family, and to village and town. University education was popular and cheap, and many of the students were very young when they went up – boys rather than men. The excellences and successes of the Scottish educational system were reflected in the enormous prestige locally and internationally of the Scottish universities and colleges, and in particular their reputation for the training in medicine, science and engineering they provided.

82 Boys at play beside the Moneypool Burn, Creetown, Stewartry of
Kirkcudbright. Photograph by A. Brown and Co. of Lanark about 1890

A McConchie of Kirkcudbright composition, possibly for the artist
A. Hornel to work from. Hornel himself took many photographs on his
Eastern tours. About 1895

84 'Glasgow Highlanders'! Donald Sinclair Morrison (b. 1848), Robert Morrison (b. 1850), Anne Morrison (b. 1853), and Jane Morrison (b. 1855). Their mother, Catherine Sinclair, came from Mull. Their father, Robert Morrison, worked for a Glasgow tobacco firm: he took the photograph with him to the U.S.A. and had it framed in New York. Photograph by Bowman of Jamaica Street, Glasgow, about 1859

86 Boys playing cricket at Murthly School, near Caputh and Dunkeld, Perthshire. 1904. Cricket was a popular game in Lowland villages and towns in the 1890s and 1900s

85 The Griffin girls, and 'Patch' (cf. plate 74)

87 The Beach, Saltcoats, Ayrshire. Everyone is covered in voluminous clothing as protection against sunshine, the sea air, and stares. It seemed even faintly daring to have bare feet! Probably a Glasgow Fair holiday crowd

88 On the Sands at Prestwick, Ayrshire, 1906. A much more lively composition than the usual beach photographer's work

89 Paddling, purportedly at
Portobello, near Edinburgh, 1907.
Photograph by M. Wane and Co.,
Edinburgh (see plate 3)

90 The Plantation, South Beach, Saltcoats. 1908. A really classical photograph

Plantation South
Beach Saltcoats.

91 Madras College, St Andrews, showing the First Prizers, July 1858. The College, founded by Dr Bell on the monitorial or 'Madras' system of school management, opened in 1833. It replaced the old grammar and burgh schools

92 Students, professors and others at the University of Edinburgh Medical
School Building – architect Dr Rowand Anderson. It was partially opened in
1880 and completed in 1888

LEISURE HOURS

93 James Richardson, the Hawick
Cornet in 1862, with some of his
supporters. Photograph by
J.Y. Hunter of Hawick

Border Traditions

The strong and genuine sense of the past and the local patriotism of many Lowland communities are most clearly illustrated in the local festivals and processions, bound up with the survival of old traditions and ceremonies, at the Common Riding celebrations in the Border Towns.

94 *Left* The crowd at the 'Snuffing' in Hawick in 1912. The Snuffin' at Kirkstyle near the Auld Brig is a public ceremony going back to the old tradition of stopping to pass the snuff-box round the drummers and pipers during the Friday morning parade

95 The procession at the Hawick Common Riding in 1904. Notice the band in the forefront

96 The Casting of the Colours at the Selkirk Common Riding in 1898. The ritual sweeping and weaving patterns of the Casting of the Burgh Standard, commemorating the bringing of the news of the disaster of Flodden, are repeated by the Incorporations of Hammermen, Souters, Weavers and Tailors and by the Colonials. Photograph by R. Clapperton of Selkirk

The Church and the People

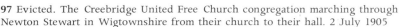

97 Evicted. The Creebridge United Free Church congregation marching through Newton Stewart in Wigtownshire from their church to their hall. 2 July 1905

Millions of middle class and working class Scots regularly attended religious services. Hundreds of thousands of the really poor and destitute did not. Those who did had to choose between the brands offered by the main Presbyterian churches, the Established Church of Scotland, the Free Church, and the United Presbyterian Church, by the Baptists, the Methodists, and the Congregationalists, by the Scottish Episcopalian and Roman Catholic Churches, and by other groups each providing their own individual interpretations of the only correct form of Christian belief and worship and organisation.

The degree of sectarian bitterness and controversy and the waste of energy and resources as a result of the machinations of groups of good and devout Christians is still all too easy to understand in much of the Central Lowlands today. The Creebridge dispute suggests something of the tensions and problems of

98 Restored. The congregation back at the Creebridge Church. 2 June 1907

he period and also of the intensely 'middle class' cultural aspirations of the respectable church goer. Respectability' was just terribly important.

Doon the Water

Dunoon and Rothesay and Brodick, and Ardrishaig and Tarbert and Campbeltown – all names with a magic of their very own in the 1880s and 1890s and 1900s for thousands of people in the West of Scotland. For men, women and children living and working in Glasgow, Paisley and industrial Lanarkshire day trips down the Clyde from the Broomielaw and Gourock to seaside resorts in the Firth were highlights of the year, to be anticipated and savoured and lingered over – an escape from the everyday grime and drudgery to magnificent steamships and equally to magnificent scenery.

99 *Left* Starting point at the Broomielaw in Glasgow

100 En route – passing the Cloch Lighthouse in Renfrewshire

101 Ardrishaig – and possibly for a coach tour to Lochgilphead, Inveraray, or Tarbert

102 An enormous crowd and amazing excitement in this photograph of the S.S. *Kinloch* at Campbeltown about 1910. The *Kinloch*, built in Glasgow in 1878 for the Campbeltown and Glasgow Steam Packet Company, was on the Gourock–Campbeltown run until she was sold in 1926 to the Channel Island Steam Packet Company

103 Rothesay, perhaps the most important and impressive Clyde resort, showing Guildford Square and the harbour with the Port Bannatyne tramcar. Some superb street furniture and seafront hotels

104 Rothesay, showing the bandstand with the inevitable military or pseudo-military band playing – 'the' centrepiece in so many holiday towns. And a very fashionable middle class or pseudo-middle class audience (it was always possible on holidays, after all, to aspire to a social status one did not normally possess)

0705 GUILDFORD SQUARE, ROTHESAY. Poulton

105 The Rothesay-Port Bannatyne Tram (Fare 2d.). Notice the splendid advertisements indicating that 'Waddell's Sausages Are The Best' and that 'Keaton's Liquor Whiskies Are The Best Scotch'. Both are remembered with affection in Glasgow

Sport and Recreation

106 St Andrews in 1888. A J. Valentine photograph of the R. and A. Club House and the Grand Hotel. Golf was by this time a growing national and international sport and leisure industry. The Royal and Ancient Golf Club goes back ultimately to the Golfing Society of 1754. A St Andrews Mechanics Golf Club was founded in 1843

107 Lawn tennis at Biggar in the late 1880s. Biggar was also a popular holiday town for visitors from Glasgow or Edinburgh. Photograph by C. Reid of Wishaw

108 Nos. 4–6 North Gardner Street, off Hyndland Road, Glasgow (with For Sale or For Let notices in windows) and tennis courts about 1904 or 1905. A lively Griffin photograph. The courts are now a bowling green

109 A Griffin photograph of curling at Hogganfield Loch, Glasgow about 1905. There were curling ponds and clubs in villages and towns all through the Lowlands

110 Lochwinnoch Cycling Club at Newton of Barr Tollhouse, Renfrewshire about 1905. An all-male cycling club (there were some mixed clubs) with their own cap badge. Vehicles include two penny farthings with their huge front wheels. Cycling was a craze from the 1880s onwards. Local militia included cycle volunteers by the 1890s, eg D Company (Newton Stewart) of the Galloway Rifle Volunteers in 1892

Holidays – A Mixed Bag

111 At Portobello, long the seaside
resort for Edinburgh, especially after
suburban trams and trains brought it
within easy reach of the city. There
are numerous (and essential) bathing
machines

112 St Andrews Rock Pool about 1900 or earlier, with the ladies posing in suitably modest bathing costumes. The onlookers are well prepared, with parasols for protection against sunstroke

113 And everyone looked forward to 'Pure Ice Cream'. A Griffin view taken on holiday in Ayrshire, probably at Prestwick

'A PLAGUE OF POSTCARDS'

114 Kennedys Pass between Lendalfoot and Girvan, Ayrshire about 1904. The by-then generally anachronistic use of N.B. (North Britain) for Scotland adds greatly to the interest and value of the card

The scale of enthusiasm for collecting amongst the Victorian and Edwardian middle class is difficult to grasp. All kinds of assorted ephemera, from music sheet covers, posters, Valentines, Christmas cards and cigarette cards to postcards were accumulated. Postcards were perhaps the most popular of all, at least between 1894 and 1914. Over 300 million cards were actually posted in Britain in 1895, over 400 million in 1900, and over 850 million in 1908. The number merely sold was much greater.

Deltiology, or the study and collecting of postcards, was not only an absorbing hobby but also, accidentally in most cases, a means of bringing together and preserving material of value for future historians. In many cases, where photographs have been lost or destroyed postcard versions can be found to fill in the gaps. Coverage for the Lowlands was massive, much greater in density and in consistency than for the Highlands, and of course Scottish firms such as Valentine and Sons of Dundee and Millar and Lang of Glasgow were leading British manufacturers and suppliers. In addition many small shops and businesses in towns and villages commissioned or obtained cards from other British and foreign concerns. Some of the best cards were printed in Prussia, Saxony and Hanover.

Postcards provide a vivid record of contemporary life and attitudes, not least of all because travelling photographers so indiscriminately recorded street scenes, people and occasions. The examples here cover rural transport, shipping, village life, disasters, picnic outings, occupations, antiquarian pursuits, and one humorous card looking at patterns of human relations (specifically, flirtation) in Motherwell — but almost every subject was tackled at one time or another.

115 Girvan harbour and the River Girvan. Notice the lady photographer. (A Valentine's Series card)

Tron Square, Dunning

26099

116 Tron Square and the thirteenth-century tower of St Serf's Church, Dunning, Perthshire, about 1904. (Valentine's)

117 Haugh of Urr village on the Old Military Road near Castle Douglas in the Stewartry of Kirkcudbright, about 1908. (Maxwell's Dalbeattie Series)

Haugh of Urr, Dalbeattie.

118 Peebles Hydropathic, built in 1878, after the fire in 1906. (Allan Smyth, Neidpath Press)

119 Possibly a Sunday School Teachers' outing in the Borders? (J. Sillars Richmond, Photographer, Galashiels)

120 A boat house in Ayrshire – a 'character' and an object for tourists to photograph

121 Draught Net Salmon Fishers at
Tongland on the River Dee near
Kirkcudbright. (Printed in Hanover
for W. McKenzie, Kirkcudbright)

C.S. KERR.

122 Wm. Buchan, the Peebles Town Clerk, holding the cauldron found at Hattonknowe, Peebles-shire, on 14 July 1904. Posted 1 September 1904. (*Peebles News*)

123 The Clyde Bridge and 'one of the most popular forms of amusement at Motherwell – come here and do likewise'. Sent to Miss M. McIntyre, 7 Whittinghame Gardens, Anniesland, Glasgow, 4 September 1908. (The Herald Series, W.H. & Co. Ltd., Glasgow)

CLYDE BRIDGE. MOTHERWELL

TO MOTHERWELL

This is one of the most popular forms of amusement at Motherwell come here & do likewise.